THE G

CHANGING THE GUARD • TROOPING THE COLOUR
THE REGIMENTS

Soldiers of the Household Division are renowned for the unique proficiency with which they carry out ceremonial duties. Yet, while upholding the traditions of the past, the Household Division has mastered the skill of modern soldiering with confidence, and their soldiers are equally at home in tanks, armoured cars or parachuting. Those men, whom you see replendent in their uniforms mounting guard or Trooping the Colour in disciplined ranks, are the same men who, in combat clothing, discharge operational duties worldwide.

The Household Division is made up of seven Regiments, comprising the Household Cavalry Regiment (The Life Guards and The Blues and Royals) and five Regiments of Foot Guards (Grenadier, Coldstream, Scots, Irish and Welsh). As soldiers they are second to none and throughout the world they are respected for their self-discipline, smartness and reliability.

ABOVE: *Her Majesty The Queen is Colonel-in-Chief of all the Guards Regiments, and is seen here in the uniform of the Grenadier Guards.*
LEFT: *The Colour is handed to the Ensign at the Trooping the Colour.*

THE LIFE GUARDS

The Uniforms

The Life Guards wear scarlet tunics, helmets with white plumes and white leather breeches. White crossbelts with a red flash-cord running down the centre are worn over the left shoulder.

The steel cuirass of breast and back plates, worn by both The Life Guards and The Blues and Royals, is the only body armour still worn by any British soldier. The present form of cuirass dates from the reign of George IV and although the 2nd Life Guards wore a black japanned form of it at a royal review in 1814, there is no evidence that it has been worn in battle since the late 17th century.

The boots are highly polished thigh boots and are still referred to as 'jackboots'. The cloak worn in winter or 'bad weather', covers not only the rider but also protects the haunches of the horse. The cloak worn by The Life Guards is red with a blue collar. The white-metal helmet, with brass ornamentation, is basically the Albert pattern helmet dating from 1842 and the helmet plume is made from horsehair.

With a proud tradition of over three centuries of service as a Body Guard to the Sovereign, The Life Guards are the senior, though not the oldest, Regiment of the British Army. At the end of the Civil War, a number of Royalists followed Prince Charles (later King Charles II) into exile and in Holland, 80 of them were organized into a body of Life Guards, of whom 20 were always on duty to guard the Royal residence or escort Charles. By the time of the Restoration of the monarchy in 1660, their number had increased to 600, organized into three troops – the King's Troop, The Duke of York's Troop and the Duke of Albemarle's Troop. A fourth troop was raised in Scotland soon after the Restoration. At this stage The Life Guards were known as The Horse Guards or Life Guard of Horse.

In 1678 a troop of Horse Grenadier Guards was formed, and a division of 'Mounted Grenadiers', containing 3 officers and 70 other ranks, was added to each cavalry troop. A 2nd or Scottish Troop of Horse Grenadiers was raised in 1702. In 1746, when the four-troop establishment of The Horse (or Life) Guards was reduced to two, the 1st and 2nd Troops of

ABOVE: *The Sovereign's Standard of The Life Guards is carried by the Sovereign's Escort on State occasions.*

RIGHT: *Life Guard Trooper in dismounted dress, without the cuirass. Trumpeters, mounted on grey horse, wear State Dress on State occasions. This Royal Livery, with its richly embroidered velvet coat, dates from the time of Charles II.*

BELOW: *The Waterloo field bugle of the 1st Life Guards.*

Horse Grenadier Guards were attached to each repectively.

In 1788 a major reorganization saw the 1st Troop of Horse Guards and the 1st Troop of Horse Grenadier Guards formed into the 1st Regiment of Life Guards, while the 2nd Troop became the 2nd Regiment of Life Guards. Known until then as 'Horse Guards' the new Regiments were now officially named Life Guards. This organization survived until 1922 when the two Regiments were amalgamated into The Life Guards.

The normal duties of The Guards after the Restoration were to find the guard for the Royal Palace at Whitehall and to provide an escort for the King. These duties of mounting the Sovereign's Life Guard and providing the Sovereign's Escort have remained to this day, the two principal functions of the mounted squadrons of the Household Cavalry.

The Life Guards have a distinguished fighting record and have participated in many of the major battles and campaigns of the British Army. They first saw action at Maestricht in

1673 and played a major part in the defeat of the Duke of Monmouth's army at Sedgemoor in 1685. In the Battle of the Boyne in 1690 they fought against the former James II and at Landen in 1695 they fought under William III, meeting the French Household Cavalry for the first time. The War of Austrian Succession, Dettingen and Fontenoy followed, and all the Napoleonic Wars, culminating at Waterloo in 1815. In 1882 a composite Regiment of The Life Guards and The Blues took part in Wolseley's campaign in Egypt – one action was the famous 'Moonlight Charge' at Kassassin. The Life Guards fought in both World Wars, earning 28 Battle Honours in the First and 21 in the Secord. During the Second World War the Guards Armoured Division was formed in which the Household Cavalry saw service in North-West Europe.

The Household Cavalry Regiment is stationed in Combermere Barracks, Windsor, its permanent duty station, where they are equipped with armoured cars. The Household Cavalry Museum is also housed here.

THE BLUES AND ROYALS

In 1969 The Royal Horse Guards (The Blues) were amalgamated with the Royal Dragoons (1st Dragoons) to form a new Regiment in the Household Cavalry, known as The Blues and Royals.

The Royal Horse Guards (the Blues) were directly descended from the Regiment of Horse raised by Cromwell in 1650. With the Restoration, King Charles II took the Regiment for his own, styling it 'The Royal Regiment of Horse'. Although forced to hand in its Standards in December 1660 by Parliamentary agitation for the disbandment of the army, the further threat to the monarchy changed the situation and Charles signed the birth certicate of the modern British Army in 1661. The new Regiment was to be commanded by Aubrey de Verre, Earl of Oxford.

The colour blue was associated with the Regiment from early days, but it was also the colour of the livery of the Earl of Oxford and the new Regiment wore blue coats from their inception in 1661. About 1690 they were nicknamed 'The Oxford Blues' to distinguish them from William III's Dutch Horse Guards. This name became stylized in 1750 as The Royal Horse Guards Blue, which was their title until 1819 when they became The Royal Horse Guards (The Blues).

ABOVE: *A Squadron Standard of The Blues and Royals.*

ABOVE RIGHT: *Departure of The Royal Horse Guards Squadron for Egypt, 1882. Watercolour by R. Simkin.*

RIGHT: *Trooper in Mounted Review Dress. The horse's saddle is covered with black sheepskin, and the metal links were a precautionary measure against a possible sword cut releasing the bridle. The Blues and Royals Officer is in mounted khaki Service Dress.*

RIGHT: *The jackboots worn by both The Blues and Royals and The Life Guards are of a pattern introduced by the Prince Regent in 1812.*

BELOW: *The crest of The Blues prior to amalgamation with the Royal Dragoons.*

The Uniforms

The Blues and Royals, like The Life Guards, wear full dress uniform when providing the Sovereign's Life Guard and on State occasions. The Blues and Royals wear blue tunics, red helmet plumes and white leather breeches. White crossbelts are worn over the left shoulder and the cuirasses and jackboots are identical to those of The Life Guards.

In 1820, as a compliment to their Colonel, the Duke of Wellington, and in consideration of their distinguished service at Waterloo in 1815, The Blues were granted the full status of Household Cavalry, until then only enjoyed by The Life Guards. Because of their status, the active service career of The Blues closely paralleled that of The Life Guards, with whom they fought side by side.

The Royal Dragoons (1st Dragoons) were, until the amalgamation, the oldest Cavalry Regiment of the Line, with their own Royal connections. Raised in 1661 as 'The Tangier Horse', the new Regiment spent twenty-two years fighting the Moors, and when it returned in 1684 it received the title 'His Majesty's Own Royal Regiment of Dragoons'.

After fighting in the War of the Spanish Succession, the War of the Austrian Succession and the Seven Years' War, the Royal Dragoons won further fame in 1794 against the French at Beaumont and Willems, followed by service in the Peninsula and Waterloo. The Regiment took part in the Charge of the Heavy Brigade at Balaclava in 1854; fought in Egypt and South Africa; served dismounted in the trenches during the First World War; and, then mechanized, fought in the Western Desert and in North-West Europe during the Second World War. In 1982 two troops of The Blues and Royals fought with distinction in the Falkland Islands.

On 1 October 1992 a union of the Household Cavalry took place and the Household Cavalry Regiment was formed, based in Windsor. Equipped with armoured vehicles, it consists of two squadrons of Life Guards and two squadrons of Blues and Royals.

The mounted element of the Household Cavalry consists of one squadron of both Life Guards and Blues and Royals and is based at Knightsbridge. It carries out the duties of The Queen's Life Guard at Whitehall daily.

THE GRENADIER GUARDS

The Uniforms

From a distance the full dress uniforms worn by the officers and men of the five Regiments of Foot Guards look identical. All non-commissioned Officers and Guardsmen wear the black bearskin cap; the scarlet tunic has a dark blue collar, epaulettes piped in white, and cuffs of dark blue and white; the dark blue trousers have a red stripe down the seam of each leg and a white leather buff belt completes the uniform. The Officers' uniforms differ slightly in that a crimson or gold sash replaces the white belt; tunic collars, epaulettes and cuffs are dark blue with gold embroidery; the bearskin cap is larger; the stripe on the trousers is wider than that worn by other ranks. Officers and Warrant Officers also have gold embroidery on the skirts and sleeve flaps of their tunics.

All ranks in the Grenadier Guards wear their tunic and cuff buttons evenly spaced. The bearskins have a white plume on the left-hand side. The 'grenade fired proper' emblem is worn on their tunic collars.

When wearing their 'blues' or Khaki Service Dress, NCOs and Guardsmen from the Regiment can be recognized by the red band around their peaked forage cap.

In 1656 Charles II, while in exile, raised a Regiment from his followers at Bruges. It was called the 'Royal Regiment of Guards' and the King appointed Lord Wentworth as the first colonel.

On the King's return to the Throne he disbanded the old Parliamentarian army and commissioned Colonel John Russell to raise another Regiment of twelve companies for his personal protection.

In 1665, following Lord Wentworth's death, both Regiments were incorporated into one, the 'King's Regiment of Foot Guards'. By 1685 the Regiment had become 'The First Regiment of Foot Guards' which it remained until 1815 when the title was changed for the last time to 'The First or Grenadier Regiment of Foot Guards'.

The actions which have built up the reputation of the Regiment over three hundred years are recorded by a total of 76 Battle Honours. Since Tangier in 1680, the Regiment has taken part in nearly every major campaign.

Under their Colonel, the Duke of Marlborough, the First Guards fought in all his great battles, and the Regiment played a

ABOVE: *The Queen's Colour of the 2nd Battalion Grenadier Guards is now carried by Nijmegen Company after the 2nd Battalion went into suspended animation in November 1994.*

RIGHT: *Captain of the Grenadier Guards in Frock Coat. Dating from the 1830s, this garment is worn only by Officers holding particular appointments.*

FAR RIGHT: *Grenadier Guardsman in Full Dress. The regimental emblem on the tunic collar also decorates the locket of the belt.*

major part in another victory over the French at Dettingen in 1743.

The First Guards were in the retreat to Corunna during the winter of 1808-09, and they remained in Spain throughout Wellington's Peninsula Campaign. At the Battle of Waterloo the Regiment defeated the Grenadiers of Napoleon's Imperial Guard. For this

ABOVE: *Grenadiers of the First Regiment of Foot Guards dislodging French troops from their fortified position before the village of Vason, at the Battle of Fontenoy, 30 April 1745.*

they were given the title 'The First or Grenadier Regiment of Foot Guards', usually shortened to Grenadier Guards. At the same time they became the first of the Guards Regiments to wear the bearskin cap.

The 3rd Battalion took part in all the battles of the Crimean War when four of the first Victorian Crosses were awarded to members of the Regiment.

The 1st Battalion Grenadier Guards was present at Kitchener's relief of Khartoum in 1898 and in the next year the 2nd and 3rd Battalions went to South Africa.

In the First World War the Regiment raised a fourth battalion and all four fought in France. Thirty-four Battle Honours were awarded and seven members of the Regiment won the Victoria Cross.

All three regular battalions fought with the British Expeditionary Force in France and Flanders at the beginning of the Second World War. After Dunkirk, three more battalions were formed. The 1st and 2nd Battalions became part of the Guards Armoured Division, while the 4th Battalion formed part of the 6th Guards Independent Tank Brigade. All three battalions fought throughout the North-

RIGHT: *The Court sword of the 1st Duke of Marlborough, Colonel of the First Guards, presented to him in 1702 by Queen Anne.*

West Europe campaign. The 3rd and 5th Battalions fought in Africa and Italy while the 6th Battalion went to Syria before joining the English Army in Tunisia. After the war the Guards Armoured Division disbanded and the Regiment reverted to three battalions until 1961, when the 3rd Battalion was placed in suspended animation.

Since the Second World War battalions of the Regiment have served worldwide including the Far East, Middle East, Africa, the Mediterranean, Central America and the European mainland. The Regiment has taken its share of tours in Northern Ireland, and has continued to have the honour of performing duties for Her Majesty The Queen when serving in London.

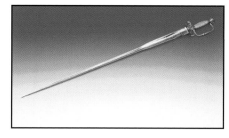

THE COLDSTREAM GUARDS

LEFT: *The Regimental Colour of the 1st Battalion Coldstream Guards.*

ABOVE: *After 'sounding the alarm' in Canada, the grateful Coldstream Guards brought Jacob the goose back to London as their regimental pet.*

ABOVE: *The Dunbar Medal, the first campaign medal to be awarded. The medal bore the head of Cromwell.*

The Coldstream Guards were raised in 1650 on the orders of Oliver Cromwell to form Colonel Monck's Regiment of Foot. They took their place in the ranks of the 'New Model Army', Britain's first regular force. For the next ten years the Regiment served with distinction and in 1660 they were still with Monck, and quartered in the small town of Coldstream on the English/Scottish border. By 1660 Cromwell had been dead for two years, Parliamentary rule had become autocratic, and life had become marked by continual political upheavals. London was the centre of most of the unrest, and in January 1660 General Monck marched his troops to the capital and set about restoring order. Although careful to avoid any direct

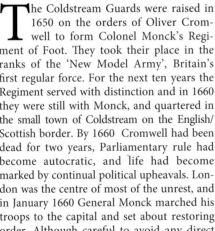

LEFT: *General Monck's snuffbox.*

RIGHT: *Officers' bearskins are taller than those of other ranks and slightly tapered in shape. The band on the Lance Corporal's forage cap is white, hence the Regiment's nickname 'The Lily-whites'.*

ABOVE: *Battle Honours on display.*

ABOVE: *The Defence of Hougoumont, 1815.*

The Uniforms
The Coldstream Guards wear red plumes on the right of their bearskin caps, and their buttons are spaced in pairs. A garter star is worn on the collar, while a rose appears on soldier's epaulettes.

BELOW: *The Waterloo Medal.*

involvement in politics, Monck and his Coldstreamers were largely responsible for securing the free elections for a new Parliament, which invited King Charles II to return to the Throne.

On his triumphal return to London the King inspected Monck's men and was most impressed with what he saw. After the Restoration, one of Parliament's first acts was to disband Cromwell's New Model Army. However, it was decreed that Monck's own Regiment of Foot and Horse should be retained to the last. By 1661 the disbandment process was well advanced; in fact Monck's Horse was actually being broken up when, together with their comrades in the Foot Regiment, they were ordered to put down a serious uprising. It was decided therefore to keep them in being, and on 14 February 1661 they were paraded on Tower Hill. They laid down their arms as soliers of the New Model Army, taking them up as King's men of the Lord General's

(Monck's new title) Regiment of Foot Guards, and the Lord General's Troop of Horse Guards. The mounted unit was later merged into The Life Guards. That historic moment dates the career of the Regiment as personal guards to the Sovereign. In 1670, after Monck's death, the Regiment was officially granted its already much used title – the Coldstream Guards.

Coldstreamers have fought many wars and kept the peace. They marched under the 1st Duke of Marlborough, and bear on their Colours, among many others, the names of Wellington's famous Peninsula battles and that of Waterloo. They have proved themselves on the South Afrcan Veldt; in Flanders; through the many campaigns of the Second World War; in Malaya; and in South Arabia. Always they have served with integrity.

THE SCOTS GUARDS

The Scots Guards have loyally and successfully served the Crown for many years, since the Regiment was first raised as a personal bodyguard for Charles I in 1642. In March of that year Charles issued a Commission addressed to Archibald, 1st Marquess of Argyll, authorizing him to raise 'a Royal Regiment of our Scottish Subjects, consisting of the number of Fifteen Hundred men'. The Regiment was sent to Ireland, but neither the King nor Argyll went with them. Instead the marquess appointed a cousin as commander in the field, and this custom of having a prince of the Blood or a distinguished soldier as Colonel, and a Lieutenant Colonel Commanding responsible for the active command of the whole Regiment, has remained.

Except for a short break in 1645, the Regiment stayed in Ireland from 1642 until 1649, when they returned to Scotland as part of Charles II's Scottish Army which was being raised to fight the English Parliamentary Forces. After the Battle of Worcester in 1651, Charles was forced to flee to Europe and Cromwell ordered the Regiment to be disbanded. Nine years later in 1660 when Charles II was restored to his throne the Regiment was

BELOW: *The Queen's Colour 2nd Battalion Scots Guards, carried by F Company, Scots Guards.*

ABOVE: *The Battle of Alma, 1854. Ensigns Lindsay and Thistlethwaite carried the Regimental Colours. For his part in this action Ensign Lindsay was awarded the Victoria Cross.*

RIGHT: *Dress coat worn by Captain the Honourable Thomas Needham, Third Guards, who served 1756-61.*

LEFT: *In Home Service Dress the bearskin cap can be replaced by a forage cap. The Piper in Full Dress wears a plaid and kilt in Royal Steward tartan. His feather bonnet bears a blue and red hackle.*

once more in being, again as part of the Scottish Army, and known as the Scottish Regiment of Foot Guards. In 1686, after various successful actions, they were brought on to the English Army's establishment and took precedence within the Foot Guards as the third Regiment. Undoubtedly their length of service, dating from 1642, ranked them as the senior Regiment, but their disbandment was adjudged to have broken the continuity, and so they took their place in the line behind the Grenadier Guards (1st) and the Coldstream Guards (2nd).

In 1695 the First Battalion won the Regiment's first Battle Honour at the Siege of Namur during the wars of Marlborough. The Regiment then underwent further name changes – in 1772 they were renamed the 'Third Regiment of Foot Guards' but, in 1831, King William gave them the unusual title 'Scots Fusilier Guards' and it was from that date that the whole Regiment wore the bearskin cap. The present title 'Scots Guards' was conferred upon them by Queen Victoria in 1877.

Although their name changed, the Regi-

The Uniforms
The Scots Guards wear the buttons on their tunics and tunic cuffs in threes. (Uniform above pre-dates regulation.) When the Regiment joined the Household Troops they required no plume, because they always stood in the centre of the line. Their collar badge is the traditional Scottish emblem, the thistle. The peaked forage cap worn by the Regiment has a diced band in red, white and blue.

ment's excellent fighting qualities remained constant throughout. They have taken part in every major war fought by Britain and in countless smaller actions. Their 92 Battle Honours, 40 of which are borne on their Colours, bear witness to fortitude and success. They also reflect how Scots Guardsmen through the ages have lived up to their ancient motto – 'Nemo Me Impune Lacessit' – 'Let No One Provoke Me with Impunity'.

THE IRISH GUARDS

ABOVE: *The Regiment Colour of the Irish Guards.*

Irishmen and their descendants have, over the centuries, built up a unique reputation as professional fighting troops. Queen Victoria recognized their achievements, and in particular their bravery, and raised her own Regiment of Irish Foot Guards in 1900.

The Micks, as the Irish Guards are popularly known, first saw action as mounted infantry in the Boar War, shortly after their formation. From their experience in that war was forged a close-knit family Regiment of

---

The Uniforms

The Irish Guards can be recognized by their four-button groupings on the tunics and sleeve cuffs. The plume worn on the right-hand side of the bearskin cap consists of 6in (15cm) of St Patrick's blue cut feathers or bristle, depending on rank. The collar badge is a shamrock which is white on Guardsmen's tunics but embroidered in silver on Officers' and Warrant Officers' tunics. The peaked forage cap worn with Home Service Dress has a green band.

Pipers wear saffron kilts with dark green tunics and their caubeen headdresses also bear a St Patrick's blue hackle or plume.

We're not so old in the Army List
But we're not so young at our trade
For we had the honour at Fontenoy
Of meeting the Guard's Brigade.

From a poem, 'The Irish Guards', by Rudyard Kipling, whose son was killed in the Irish Guards in 1915.

RIGHT: *Enlistment poster for the Irish Guards, 1901. Requirements were for men between the ages of 18 and 25.*

FAR RIGHT: *The Irish Guards, like all Guards Regiments, carry out ceremonial and operational duties with the same efficiency. They are all highly trained in the use of modern weaponry.*

RIGHT: *The 1st Battalion Irish Guards are led by their mascot Domhnall, an Irish wolfhound, on St Patrick's Day. Brian Boru, the first mascot of the Regiment, 1902-10, was named after the famous king of Ireland, and subsequent dogs have been named after Irish heroes.*

exceptional professional qualities whose gallantry and fighting spirit was to be recognized in the ensuing two World Wars by the awards of six Victoria Crosses. During the course of these wars the Regiment fought in practically every major battle. In the Second World War they displayed their exceptional versatility by fighting in such varied roles as Infantry, Armoured, Paratroop and Commando soldiers; their proudest moment amongst many was their service in North Africa and Italy under the command of that outstanding soldier and much-loved Irish Guardsman,

Field Marshal The Earl Alexander of Tunis, Fifth Colonel of the Irish Guards.

Each year on St Patrick's Day shamrock is distributed to each Guardsman in a Royal tradition dating back to 1901. Originally given by Queen Alexandra, then for many years by Queen Elizabeth the Queen Mother, this duty is now graciously performed by The Princess Royal.

A unique feature of the Irish Guards is that they are the only Regiment in the Household Division to have a mascot to lead them on parade. Their mascot is an Irish Wolfhound.

THE WELSH GUARDS

The Welsh Regiment of Foot Guards was formed on 26 February 1915 by order of His Majesty King George V. The number of Welshmen transferring from other Regiments made it possible for the 1st Battalion to mount Guard at Buckingham Palace three days later on St David's Day.

Following six months of intensive training, the 1st Battalion fought their first battle at

BELOW: *The Queen's Colour 1st Battalion Welsh Guards.*

BOTTOM: *The Welsh Guards on active service in the Falkland Islands in 1982.*

The Uniforms
The Welsh Guards wear on the left of the bearskin cap a plume, coloured white-green-white, made of cut feathers or bristle. Being the fifth Regiment of Foot Guards the buttons on tunic, cuff and skirt are in groups of five. Both the collar and epaulettes carry the leek, which was used as a Welsh emblem as early as the seventh century and has connections with St David.

Loos on 27 September 1915, and fought in France and Flanders for the rest of the First World War as part of the Guards Division.

A second battalion was formed in 1939, and fought at Boulogne in 1940, while the 1st Battalion was in Belgium as part of the British Expeditionary Force. A third service battalion was raised during the Second World War and fought in North Africa and Italy. Meanwhile the 1st and 2nd Battalions formed part of the Guards Armoured Division; the 1st Battalion as mechanized infantry and the 2nd Battalion as an Armoured Reconnaissance Battalion. The 1st and 2nd Battalions, working together, were the first British troops to re-enter Brussels on 3 September 1944, after an advance of a hundred miles in one day, in what was exuberantly descibed at the time as 'an armoured dash unequalled for speed in this or any other war'.

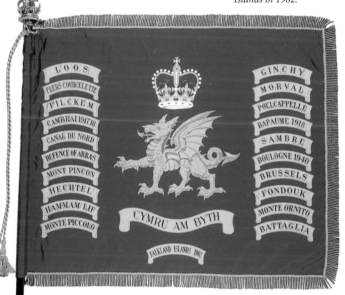

ABOVE: *Drummer of the Welsh Guards in Full Dress.*

RIGHT: *Enlistment poster for the Welsh Guards, 1915.*

CYMRU AM BYTH

WELSH GUARDS

GOOD PAY

SOUND COMRADESHIP

RECRUITS

Are now wanted for the above Regiment.

QUALIFICATIONS.

Welsh parentage on one side at least or domiciled in Wales or Monmouth or men with Welsh surnames. Good Character

Height : 5ft. 7ins. and upwards.   Age : 18 to 25 years.

TERMS OF SERVICE : 3 YRS. WITH COLOURS & 9 YRS. IN RESERVE OR FOR THE PERIOD OF THE WAR

Apply to the nearest Recruiting Officer or Barracks, and say you want to join the WELSH GUARDS.

GOD SAVE THE KING

Y MAE EISIEU

GWYR IEUAINC

o gymeriad da i wasanaethu yn y Gatrawd uchod.

Rhieni Cymraeg gwyr ei cartrefi yn Cymru neu enwau (surnames) Cymraeg.

Oedran: 18 i 25 mlynedd, ag uchder 5ft. 7ins. a drossodd.

Telera'r gwasanaeth neu'r ymrwymiad yw 3 mlynedd gyda'r fyddin a 9 mlynedd fel Nellduwyr (Reserves).

EXCELLENT TRAINING

ACTIVE SERVICE

GELLIR YMRWYMO HYD DIWEDD Y RHYFEL

DUW GADWO'R BRENIN.

Shortly after the war the 3rd Battalion was disbanded and the 2nd Battalion placed in suspended animation. The 1st Battalion has since taken part in excerises all over the world. It has seen active service in Palestine, the Canal Zone of Egypt, Aden, Cyprus and Northern Ireland.

The Welsh Guards took part in the Falklands Campaign in 1982 and individual Guardsmen have served in other campaigns.

CHANGING THE GUARD

The History of the Ceremony

From the reign of Henry VII until the Civil War, the responsibility of guarding the person of the Sovereign rested with the Body Guard of the Yeomen of the Guard. During the Civil War, Charles I was gurded by loyal troops, while Charles II, when in exile, was protected by his Life Guards. From the Restoration onwards, the daily protection of the Sovereign became increasingly the duty of The Life Guards and the three original Regiments of Foot Guards, and it still remains the responsibility of the Household Division. Today, The Queen has a number of homes, both official and private. However, it is only at the London palaces and at Windsor and Edinburgh Castles that a guard is mounted.

In Stuart times, **Whitehall Palace** was the official Royal residence, having been taken over by Henry VIII in 1529, but it was largely destroyed by fire in 1698. St James's Palace thereafter became the official Royal residence, the Foot Guards taking up duties there, although The Life Guards continued to mount the Guard at what remained of Whitehall Palace. Even after the Admiralty Arch was built, Queen Victoria ruled that the Horse Guards Arch should remain the official entrance to the Royal palaces and the mounted guard at Whitehall is still maintained as The Queen's Life Guard.

ABOVE: *The St James's Palace detchment of the Old Guard marches through the Centre Gate of Buckingham Palace. The Ensign carries The Queen's Colour.*

LEFT: *The New Guard enters Ambassadors Court, St James's Palace. This painting, c.1750, shows the Band, Corps of Drums and St James's Palace detachment found by the First Regiment of Foot Guards.*

ABOVE: *The New Guard, here formed by the Scots Guards, dresses by the right in the Forecourt of Buckingham Palace.*

Since it became the official residence of the Sovereign in 1698, **St James's Palace** has remained the centre of the Court, and foreign ambassadors are still accredited to the Court of St James's. Of the two detachments which mount in the Forecourt of Buckingham Palace and form The Queen's Guard for the day, the St James's Palace detachment is therefore the senior, and it is at St James's that the Captain of The Queen's Guard establishes his headquarters and where the Colour is lodged.

Buckingham Palace was purchased for George III in 1762. The first reigning Sovereign to live there was Queen Victoria, and it became the permanent London residence of the Royal Family after her accession in 1837. It is in the Forecourt of Buckingham Palace that the Regiments of Foot Guards now mount The Queen's Guard. When seen marching to and from the ceremony, The Queen's Guard is in three main groups. First comes a Regimental Band with a Corps of Drums, then the St James's Palace detachment including the Ensign, who carries the Colour, and finally the Buckingham Palace detachment.

Where to see Guard Changings

Daily in summer (unless very wet). Alternate days in autumn and winter. (If wet, why not visit The Guards Museum.)

St James's Palace. The Senior detachment of The Queen's Guard forms up at 11 a.m. prior to marching to Buckingham Palace.

•

Buckingham Palace. At 11.30 a.m. the New Guard marches into the Palace Forecourt and the ceremony begins.

•

Whitehall. The New Guard of The Queen's Life Guard arrives at Horse Guards Arch at 11 a.m. (10 a.m. on Sundays).

•

Tower of London. At 9.50 p.m. each evening the 'Ceremony of the Keys' takes place.

•

Windsor Castle. Guard mounting at 11.30 a.m. (days vary).

CHANGING THE GUARD AT BUCKINGHAM PALACE

At 11a.m. the St James's Palace detachment of the Old Guard forms up in Friary Court at St James's Palace. After inspection by the Captain of The Queen's Guard, the Drummers beat the call 'The Point of War' as the Colour is brought on. Then, led by their Corps of Drums, the St James's detachment marches off via Stable Yard Gate and proceeds along The Mall to Buckingham Palace.

Meanwhile the Buckingham Palace detachment of the Old Guard falls in and is inspected. The detachment then marches to the centre of the Palace Forecourt to await the arrival of the remainder of the Old Guard.

Entering the Forecourt by the South Centre Gate, the St James's detachment forms up on the right of the Buckingham Palace Guard. The Old Guard is then complete and awaits the arrival of the New Guard.

At 11.30 the New Guard, led by their Regiment Band and Corps of Drums, marches into the Palace Forecourt via the North Centre Gate. The New Guard marches to a central position, then executes a left-form and halts facing the Old Guard. Supervised by the Drill Sergeant, the New Guard then dresses by the right, the Band and Corps of Drums forming up behind the Guard.

ABOVE: *Ensign of the Old Guard and New Guard patrol with the Colours during the Changing the Guard ceremony.*

LEFT: *Guards posted on sentry duty at Buckingham Palace receive orders for the day.*

The New Guard then advances in slow time towards the Old Guard and halts. Both Guards present arms. During this present-arms the Ensign do not lower the Colours.

Both Guards having paid each other military compliments, the Captains of the Guard bring their swords from the salute to the carry position and march towards each other to carry out the symbolic ceremony of handing over the Palace Keys. The responsibility for the security and safety of the Palace and its occupants thus passes from the Old Guard to the New Guard.

The officers of the Buckingham Palace detachments both Guards salute the Senior Captain on parade with their swords and, with the Senior NCOs, proceed to the guardroom to hand over and take over respectively.

ABOVE: *A Drum Major on duty at the Guard Changing ceremony.*

Having done this they report once more to the Senior Captain. During the hand-over the Ensigns, with the Colours, patrol at the rear.

Officers with no direct involvement in the ceremony fall out and walk up and down informally on the west side of the Guards.

The Captains of the Guard go into the Palace to receive any special orders for the day and then rejoin the main ceremony. When each new sentry is posted, complete orders are read to him by the Corporal.

Having posted new sentries at Buckingham Palace the relieved sentries march into the Forecourt and complete the Old Guard.

At 12.05 the Guards are re-formed and brought to attention. The Old Guard advances until level with the Centre Gate, at which point it right-forms, becoming a column of route. Compliments are paid to the Old Guard's Colour by the New Guard, and are returned. Once clear of the Centre Gate the Old Guard, led by the Regiment Band and Corps of Drums, right-wheels and then breaks into quick time. The Old Guard is now on its way back to barracks.

The New Guard now slopes arms at the order of the Captain. It is henceforth referred to as the Queen's Guard. The Buckingham Palace detachment stands fast as the St James's Palace detachment turns right. The Queen's Guard is thus split and the St James's detachment marches off. At Friary Court the Colour is marched off and lodged in the St James's Palace guardroom. Meanwhile the Buckingham Palace detachment marches off to its own guardroom.

TROOPING THE COLOUR

The History of the Ceremony

Every year, in June, on the day chosen as the Sovereign's Official Birthday, Horse Guards Parade witnesses a ceremony which has been described as the greatest parade of all. This is the Sovereign's Birthday Parade, or the ceremony of Trooping the Colour in the presence of Her Majesty The Queen, the Colonel-in-Chief of all seven Regiments of the Household Division. However, few of the many millions of people who watch the ceremony annually fully appreciate the original purpose of a basically simple exercise, which has since become overlaid with the splendour of a major State occasion.

In the early days of land warfare, flags or Colours were used by military leaders as rallying or assembly points for their followers in battle. As the organization of military forces became more complex, sub-units of the main force, such as the company, began to have their own distinguishing device, although, from about the beginning of the 18th century, battalion Colours mostly replaced company Colours.

Because of their importance in battle, it was necessary to ensure that every soldier could recognize his own unit's flag or Colour, and it became the practice to carry, or 'troop', the Colour down the ranks at the end of the day's

ABOVE: *A Scots Guards Officer at the Sovereign's Birthday Parade.*

march and to escort it to the place where it would be lodged for the night. The following morning the Colour would be escorted from the billet to take its place within the ranks of the battalion. As a result of these ceremonies, known originally as 'Lodging the Colour', the Colour gradually began to lose its strictly operational associations and to become an object of reverence which embodies the spirit and traditions of the unit in question.

Following the Restoration of King Charles II in 1660, every garrison town was the scene of a daily Guard-mounting parade which began with the main Guard parading through the principal streets. By the mid-18th century, whenever the Sovereign was in residence in the district, a Captain's Guard was mounted over him and the daily parade would include a ceremony of 'Trooping the Colour'. These parades were similar to those which still take place on certain days in May, when The Queen's Guard mounts from Horse Guards.

It eventually became the custom to find the Public Duties, or Guard, on the Sovereign's Birthday from the flank companies of the whole Brigade of Guards, so that every Regiment could share in the gratuity given by the Sovereign on that day to men on guard duties. Trooping the Colour on the Sovereign's Birthday grew out of these two customs.

ABOVE: *Her Majesty The Queen watches the march past of Household troop from a dais.*

LEFT: *Her Majesty The Queen rides to Horse Guards Parade in an ivory-mounted phaeton made for Queen Victoria.*

BELOW: *The Sovereign's Birthday Parade at which the Trooping the Colour ceremony takes place is held annually by the Household Division at Horse Guards Parade.*

TROOPING THE COLOUR

The Sovereign's Birthday Parade

The Birthday Parade usually includes six Guards of the Foot Guards, each comprising 3 Officers and 70 other ranks. Nos. 1 to 5 Guards form up on the west side of Horse Guards Parade facing Horse Guards Archway, while No. 6 Guard forms up at right angles to the other five. The Massed Bands, Pipes and Drums of the Household Division form up in front of the

garden of No.10 Downing Street. The Queen's Colour is then posted in front of No. 6 Guard. The parade is dressed and, when the line is formed, the officers fall in.

At 11 a.m. The Queen arrives from Buckingham Palace, attended by the Royal Procession and escorted by the Sovereign's Escort of the Household Cavalry. As Her Majesty arrives at the Saluting Base, she is received with a Royal Salute, the Bands playing the National anthem.

The Queen inspects the parade, and then returns to the Saluting Base, while the Guards stand at ease.

The parade is called to attention and is given the command 'Troop'. The Massed Bands, Pipes and Drums advance in slow time towards the Colour, then return to their original position in quick time, one Drummer leaving and marching towards the Escort for the Colour.

The Escort now marches to the centre of the parade ground and halts facing the Colour. The entire parade comes to attention and the

ABOVE: *Silver Stick, Officer commanding Household Cavalry.*

LEFT: *The Brigade Major leading the Royal Procession.*

BELOW: *The Escort for the Colour trooping the Colour.*

LEFT: *The Drummer uncasing the Colour. The Colour will later be trooped through the ranks.*

RIGHT: *On State occasions the Drum Majors of the Foot Guards wear State Dress. The livery is similar to that of the Household Cavalry, but with white gaiters and a gold-fringed crimson apron.*

Colour is handed over to the Ensign. When the Escort presents arms to receive the Colour, the four NCOs at the flanks turn outwards and port arms, symbolically barring access to the Colour from all directions.

The Colour is now trooped from left to right down the entire line of Guards. As the Escort reaches its original position, it faces to the front in line with the other Guards.

The Guards now form up and march past Her Majesty, first in slow and then in quick time. The Colour is brought to the front of the Escort and is lowered in Salute as the Ensign passes The Queen. When each Guard reaches its original position, it marks time until the whole line is re-formed, at which point the music reaches a crescendo and the whole line is ordered to halt.

It is now the turn of the Household Cavalry to pay their respects to The Queen. As the Foot Guards present arms, each Division rides past Her Majesty, first at the walk and then at the trot, the Standard being dipped as it passes The Queen. The final order is given, 'Royal Salute – Present Arms', and the National Anthem is played.

The six Guards re-form in Divisions for the march to Buckingham Palace, the leading Division being the St James's Palace detachment and the rear Division the Buckingham Palace detachment of The Queen's Guard for the day. Her Majesty takes up position at the head of The Queen's Guard.

At Buckingham Palace the Old Guard has already formed up for the normal Guard Mounting ceremony. Her Majesty proceeds to the Centre Gate. The two detachments of The Queen's Guard form up opposite the Old Guard. The remaining Foot Guards and, finally, the Sovereign's Escort then march past Her Majesty. The Queen is then driven into the Palace, passing between the Old and New (or Queen's) Guards.

BELOW: *The Blues and Royals ride past Her Majesty The Queen.*

GUARD DUTIES

The Tower of London

The Regiment finding The Queen's Guard for the day at Buckingham Palace also provides the Guard for the Tower of London. There is no ceremonial Guard Mounting parade in the Tower.

During the day, two ceremonial sentries are mounted, one outside The Queen's House, the other immediately outside the guard-room. These sentries are changed every hour in winter and every two hours in summer.

Every evening at 10 p.m., one of the oldest military ceremonies in the world, the traditional 'Ceremony of the Keys' takes place. At 9.50 p.m. an Escort – comprising the Sergeant of the Guard, a Guardsman whose duty it is to carry the lantern, and two armed Guardsmen – parade under the Bloody Tower Archway. The Chief Yeoman Warder, in scarlet coat and Tudor bonnet, carrying in one hand a candle lantern and in the other The Queen's Keys, joins the group and hands his lantern to the Guardsman. The party

RIGHT: *The Chief Warder ceremonially locks the Tower of London escorted by the Guard at the Ceremony of the Keys.*

BELOW: *The Life Guards and The Blues and Royals change the Guard at Whitehall. The two Regiments provide The Queen's Life Guard.*

moves to the Middle Tower, where it halts while the Chief Yeoman Warder locks the gate. This procedure is repeated at the Byward Tower. Along the route, all guards and sentries salute The Queen's Keys.

As the Escort to the Keys returns along Water Lane, the sentry at the Bloody Tower issues the challange: 'Halt, who comes there?' The Chief Yeoman Warder replies: 'The Keys'. The sentry asks: 'Whose Keys?' whereupon the Chief Yeoman Warder declares: 'Queen Elizabeth's Keys'. The sentry then says: 'Pass, Queen Elizabeth's Keys, and all's well'.

Both the Main Guard and the Escort present arms as the Chief Yeoman Warder, raising his Tudor bonnet, proclaims: 'God preserve Queen Elizabeth', to which all reply: 'Amen'. The Drummer sounds the Last Post on the bugle and the ceremony comes to a close as the clock chimes ten. The Chief Yeoman Warder then carries the Keys to the Resident Governor at The Queen's House and The Guard is dismissed.

Windsor Castle

The Battalion of Foot Guards stationed at Windsor normally provides the daily Guard at Windsor Castle. The Guard Mounting ceremony takes place at 11 a.m. and is held in the Quadrangle if the Court is in residence or in Engine Court should there be a likelihood of damage to the grass in the Quadrangle. During the summer months when the Court is not in residence, Guard Mounting takes place on the lawn on Castle Hill, and in winter on the parade ground outside the Guard Room near Henry VIII's Gateway. When The Queen is in residence the Guard comprises one Officer, five NCOs, one Drummer, and 21 Guardsmen; on other occasions it comprises one Officer, five NCOs, one Drummer and 15 Guardsmen. Here, too, the ceremony is a smaller version of that held at Buckingham Palace. Sentries are posted at various points, including the Advanced Gate, facing Queen Victoria's statue; at St George's Gate, south of the Round Tower; at the George IV Gate, looking down the Long Walk; in the Quadrangle; at the Brunswick Tower at the eastern end of the North Terrace; and outside the guardroom. The double sentries at the Advanced, St George's and George IV Gates are reduced to single sentries when Her Majesty is not in residence.

ABOVE: *A Coldstream Guardsman on sentry duty at Windsor Castle.*

ABOVE: *A mounted sentry of The Blues and Royals at Whitehall.*

Changing the Queen's Life Guard at Whitehall

The New Guard rides down The Mail on its way to the Guard Mounting at Whitehall. This Guard mounts daily in the Front Yard or on Horse Guards at Whitehall and is provided alternately by The Life Guards and The Blues and Royals. The whole force, quartered at Hyde Park Barracks, is known as the Household Cavalry Mounted Regiment.

The Old and New Guards are drawn up facing each other, having saluted the respective Standards. Sentries from the New Guard rein back and head towards the guardroom. As they pass both Standards they give an 'eyes-left'.

The two mounted sentries, whose boxes face Whitehall, are posted by the Corporal-of-Horse. He also posts the dismounted sentries and marches the sentries of the Old Guard to the guardroom.

Having re-formed, the Old Guard receives and gives salutes to the New Guard, now The Queen's Life Guard, before moving off back to barracks. The Queen's Life Guard dismounts and files into the guardroom.

ACTIVE SERVICE

Men from the Regiments of the Household Division have taken part in nearly every war or internal security operation in which the British Army has been involved during the past 330 years. Their fighting qualities, tenacity and courage have been an example for all to see. Their system of training, with its discipline and high standards, has remained at the heart of their great tradition.

In modern times members of the Household Division have displayed their fighting skill in jungle, desert and mountain, in freezing cold and steaming heat. They have proved adaptable and flexible as shown by their conversion to armour in the Second World War and the formation of the famous Guards Armoured Division and 6th Guards Tank Brigade.

They have applied common sense, sound judgement and fighting skill to the many difficult internal security operations such as Cyprus, Palestine, Aden, Malaya, Borneo and the Falklands Campaign in which they have taken part. More recently they have played their full part in Northern Ireland.

Within the Household Division there are Regiments equipped with armoured cars, Challenger tanks, Warrior armoured personnel carriers and many other vehicles.

All Regiments have the most modern equipment in the form of weapons, radio sets, radar and night viewing equipment. Many members are parachute trained.

ABOVE: *A soldier from the Irish Guards on patrol in Basra, Iraq.*

LEFT: *Members of the Household Cavalry Regiment, Prince William's former squadron, on patrol in Afghanistan.*

RIGHT: Soldiers from the 1st Battalion Coldstream Guards stand with their weapons in front of a Jackal patrol vehicle during a training exercise on Salisbury Plain as they prepare to deploy to Afghanistan.

BELOW: The MILAN Anti Tank weapon being fired on a range.

THE MUSICIANS

Today the seven Regiments of the Household Division all have bands of highly accomplished musicians, each directed by a commissioned Officer. The bands of the five Regiments of Foot Guards each contain some 46 musicians, while those of the Household Cavalry Regiment are about 34 strong. In addition, each battalion of Foot Guards has its own Corps of Drums comprising six to eight drummers and percussionists and about a dozen pipers, while the Scots and Irish Guards also have some 25 pipers. These Corps of Drums and the pipers have always been on a different footing from other regimental bandsmen. They were originally employed to convey their commander's orders by means of their instruments, besides playing routine calls or tunes, and raising the spirits of their men as they went into action. They are thus on the establishment of their battalions, rather than being part of the regimental band.

As early as the 17th century The Life Guards had a code of trumpet calls and drum signals for conveying orders. For a long time these were the only instruments used. The trumpet is traditionally a 'Royal' instrument, used to herald Royal processions and entrances, and its fanfares still perform this role on State occasions and ceremonial parades. The trumpeters of the Household Cavalry have, in fact, always had a dual function. Whenever The Queen or another member of the Royal Family is present, they are State musicians wearing State Dress, as are the Drum-Majors of the Foot Guards; otherwise they are normal regimental musicians.

ABOVE *The trumpeters and drummers of the Household Cavalry rehearse for the Sovereign's Birthday Parade. The stately drum horse is that of The Blues and Royals.*

LEFT: *The massed bands of the Guards.*

ABOVE: *The Scots Guards are led by their pipers as they change Guard at Buckingham Palace.*